CAPTAIN COOK IN NEW SOUTH WALES

CAPTAIN COOK IN NEW SOUTH WALES

JAMES BONWICK

ISBN: 978-93-5614-629-7

Published: 1901

LECTOR HOUSE LLP
E-MAIL: info@lectorhouse.com

CAPTAIN COOK IN
NEW SOUTH WALES

OR
THE MYSTERY OF NAMING BOTANY BAY

BY

JAMES BONWICK, F.R.G.S.

AUTHOR OF "GEOGRAPHY OF AUSTRALIA,"
"LAST OF THE TASMANIANS,"
ETC., ETC.

1901

CONTENTS

CAPTAIN COOK IN NEW SOUTH WALES

This being the age of criticism, and not the time of taking for granted as a fact whatever one had heard from book or speech, an investigation of the story of Cook's Discovery of New South Wales may neither be unwelcome nor unexpected.

The story must have been deemed of consequence, when the Admiralty was willing to pay Dr. Hawkesworth six thousand guineas, or pounds, as reported, to write the account of that voyage in H.M.S. *Endeavour*.

Though even after its appearance some doubts were expressed as to its propriety, or even veracity, yet some allowance was made for professional jealousies, as well as for the paucity of information upon Australian matters, and the want of means either to substantiate or reject the assertions of the writer.

Objection was taken to the literary mode adopted. The author chose to make the narrative in the form of a personal record of events. The Captain was represented as speaking of himself, saying, "I saw," or "I did," &c. It was asserted by critics that to accomplish this personal mode of narration, there would necessarily arise some difficulties in the rearrangement of his sources of history. Was there not a little temptation in the adoption of that plan to alter, repress, or exaggerate facts, or even to invent trivial matters for accommodation?

The book had a wonderful sale, and no great amount of hostile remarks. Dr. Hawkesworth's death, so soon after the publication, disarmed those ready to question. Cook's fellow-voyagers, Banks, Matra, and the officers of the *Endeavour*, were either silent, absent, or unqualified to speak. Thoughtful men did inquire into the sources of the writer's information, their extent, and authenticity. The singular dispersion, loss, or destruction of such sources were fresh causes of embarrassment. Mr., afterwards Sir Joseph, Banks, is said to have declared that he furnished no assistance to the Editor.

Here it may be at once announced that this inquiry into the published Voyage of the *Endeavour* through the pen of Dr. Hawkesworth, has little to do with Cook as a man and a navigator. The story was written by a literary man, commanded or selected, and the Grand Old Sailor who has for so long a time engrossed the affectionate interest and respectful regard of all Australians, as the discoverer, or, if you will, the re-discoverer of the eastern side of New Holland, will not suffer in our esteem by the criticism of a book about the voyage.

Though that side happened to be that chosen for the New South Wales early settlement, yet the people of South Australia, Western Australia, Queensland, New Zealand, and Tasmania, with its emigrating offspring of Port Phillip—now Victoria—lands first seen by Hollanders a century or more before Cook was born, have the like reverence as those of Sydney for the indirect cause of British extension in those Southern Colonies.

Canada is as indebted to the scientific pilot of the St. Lawrence for the addition of its western woodlands to the British Empire, as the continent and islands of Australia may be to the Yorkshire mariner on the Pacific, for their occupation by our countrymen under the Crown.

No one who reads with pleasure the Voyage of the *Resolution*, about which no doubts ever existed, will think the less of James Cook, because the narrative of the *Endeavour* had the misfortune to be prepared, in his absence, by a less capable historian. As the worthy Captain always candidly acknowledged his inability, from defective education, and from absorption in seamanlike pursuits from his early boyhood, to tell his own tale, we naturally wonder how Dr. Hawkesworth compiled the adventurous voyage of the *Endeavour*.

The natural answer would be *the Logs and Journals of the voyagers*. Cook himself wrote very little, but there are now in existence several Journals attributed to him, or written under his direction. Those in the so-called *Queen's* Log, the *Admiralty* Log, the British *Museum* Log (presented by Banks), and that one in the possession of the Hudson family at Sunderland. There is, also, in the British Museum one precious *Autograph Log* whose records included the Australian portion of the voyage, in *Cook's handwriting*, and the only one extant which we expect can claim to be written by himself. Others are *reported* copies, by ships' clerks, sent home from Java.

What great differences may be observed even in these Logs? or, in what way does the official "Cook's Voyage" differ from any of them?

The most important points are those affecting the names of Botany Bay and New South Wales, with the language used in taking *possession* of the new Territory.

We have next to consider whether there are Logs remaining which were compiled by officers of the ship *Endeavour*.

A few years ago, behind some old wainscotting in the Deptford Government Victualling Yard, were discovered several *Logs* of the interesting ship, which are now safely preserved in the admirably conducted Public Record Office, Chancery Lane.

Do these *veritable* Logs and Journals throw any light upon the disputed questions respecting *Botany Bay* and *New South Wales*? The plain unvarnished tale of seamen, though oftentimes copied from each other, yet evidently written down at the period of the occurrence of events, may be set against the much varied accounts attributed to Cook himself, and in copies recorded to have been sent home from Java, where so many of the crew were sick.

But these copies were, apparently, made by the same transcribers, and done upon the same plan. There were blank spaces left for the *day* and *date*, with other spaces for the after insertion of the *locality* visited. It is not a little singular that our navigator should allow these Logs to be sent forth in so incomplete a state. It is not to be wondered that, if *en route*, or upon arrival in England, such copies should have these spaces more or less filled up, according to order, or to the fancy of the copyist.

We are thus prepared for the remarkable aspect of one called after its salesman, Mr. Corner, and now in Sydney's custody.

I had three opportunities, as a supposed expert, of examining that *Log*. I pointed out, in a personal interview with a distinguished Admiralty authority, my reasons for doubt as to its authenticity as a genuine *Cook*.

Corner's Log has side references in a hand differing from that in the text. The *days* named are clearly written by another party, and in red ink. The first copyist never ventured to name place or date, but left the open spaces to be filled by another. This Log names both *Point Hicks* and *Cape Howe*, unknown in earlier copies of the voyage chronicles.

There is some reason to think that Corner's document may have served as one of the authorities with Dr. Hawkesworth. Thus, it records "the bay which I called Edgecombe Bay," while the published work says "the bay I called Edgecombe Bay." Corner has it, of a native woman, "had nothing to cover her nudities"; but the author states "both were stark naked." In cases, the penknife was used: as, *Iron Head* was altered to *Cape Cleveland*, and both *Rockingham* and *Halifax* Bays were afterthoughts, judging from the former erasures being unsuccessfully performed.

The Logs of the *Endeavour* could not have troubled the authors of "Cook's Voyage" over much, discrepancies appearing so often between them (the supposed medium of information) and the printed volume; so much absurd or such unnecessary matters being introduced, with so large an extent of imagination employed.

These supposed Journalistic sources being frequently absent, the Doctor was treated by some as a mere romancer. It is singular that, while the assertion was repeated that he regulated his descriptions by the Journals, nothing is ever said as to what became of them, and the very names of the writers are not mentioned. Dalrymple, the great naval historian, declared at the first that Dr. Hawkesworth had not collated *all* the Journals, "as these indubitably prove"; adding, "there are many Journals he never once looked into." Dalrymple evidently knew something of them, and challenged Hawkesworth to give a list of the Journals he had incorporated.

The simple fact that the Doctor dwells so much upon *Botany Bay* and *New South Wales*, places *never* mentioned by the great majority of *Logs* in our present possession, shows singular carelessness, or a doggedness in maintaining a personal conviction wanting confirmation. The *Monthly Review* of August, 1773, admits the confusion of a composite style in having each Commander telling his own story, with the Doctor's reflections being intermixed, so that the result is a medley of seaman and philosopher, employing indiscriminately the "language of the *Log* book and the *Portico*."

COOK'S LOGS.

These are of two ages, determined by their contents. Those which introduce *Stingray Bay* instead of *Botany Bay*, and which mention neither *New South Wales* nor *New Wales* pertain to the primitive order, executed while on the voyage, like the logs of the Lieutenant, the Gunner, the Boatswain, the Master's-Mate, &c.

Of this class there are two in the British Museum, one of which (a copy) was presented there by Cook's friend, Sir Joseph Banks, and the other, containing only a portion of the voyage, written in Cook's *own hand* as seen in his own official letters. Outside the Museum only one *Log* can be identified as genuine; being, though a copy, signed by Cook, and declared to be a present from the Captain himself to his friend and patron, Sir Hugh Palliser, and ever since remaining in the custody of the Palliser family.

These three *Logs* know nothing of *New South Wales* nor *Botany Bay*.

Several other *Logs*, purporting to have been sent home later by the Captain, have filled up spaces with the names of *New South Wales*, *Port Jackson*, and *Botany Bay*, all unknown to Captain Cook or Lieutenant Hickes.

It does not yet appear that Dr. Hawkesworth, Editor of the Voyage of the *Endeavour*, had access to any *original* Cook's Log or Journal. Sir Joseph Banks is said to have repudiated supplying the Doctor with any material. Cook and his Lieutenant were absent on another voyage, nor does any other person connected with the voyage, as Dr. Solander and James Matra, appear to have communicated information. The Editor was perforce driven to make use of other and less reliable sources for his story, framed, as it was, on the model of a personal narrative—the Adventures of Captain Cook.

That Journal of Cook's presented by Sir Joseph Banks, and still to be examined by a visitor at the Museum, is numbered among the "Additional Manuscripts" as *8959*. It is well bound, bearing at the back the words *Mus. Brit.—ex legato—Banks, Bart.—8959*. The priceless copy in Cook's own hand, well written, if not always correctly spelled, is numbered *27,885* in the Museum Catalogue, and contains on a fly-sheet at the beginning the statement that the *Log* was purchased of Messrs. Borne on 13th of May, 1868.

Cook's own Journal is known generally as the *Autograph*, from bearing his correct signature. The transcriber of the *Endeavour Log, 8959*, possessed by Banks, wrote in a neat but rather small hand, very different from Cook's. It is, as might be well expected of such an early Journal, though passing through Banks's hands, ignorant of the existence of a *Botany Bay*, but refers to *Skeats* rather than *Stingray*, after which Cook's *Autograph Log* names the Bay. It has neither *Point Hickes* nor *Cape Howe* as in later days, though indicating *Pidgeon's House Hill* and *Mount Dromedary*. Yet we have *smoaks* and *smooks* as in Cook's own hand work.

THE PALLISER LOG.

The Palliser Log, presented by Cook himself to his old American Commander and patron, Admiral Sir Hugh Palliser, was examined by me in Sunderland, when invited there by its owner for some days, Mr. R. W. Hudson, the northern shipowner. His lady, a Palliser, assured me the book had never been out of the possession of the family since Cook's gift.

I read therein:—

> "This Book was a Present from Captain Cook to Sir Hugh Palliser, containing his Logg from the 27th May, 1768, to the 11th June, 1771, during his voyage on board the *Endeavour* Bark, sent to make observations on the Transit of Venus in the South Seas, and afterwards to make discoveries in the Southern Hemisphere."

The book was bound in red morocco, gold bordered, with a fancy back, and marked:—

> "Cook's Logg Book, 1768, 1769, 1770, 1771."

Though not, as I saw at once, wholly in Cook's handwriting, the record had no knowledge either of *Botany Bay* or of *New South Wales*, but had the Cook's style of spelling, as: "*severell smokes* were seen," and "*saw smokes* upon the shore." What was afterwards known as *Botany Bay* is there called "*Sting Ray Harbour.*"

Apart from the Museum Logs, this one is undoubtedly the best authenticated *Cook's Log*.

THE DEPTFORD LOGS.

Among the profound *Endeavour* mysteries must be cited the extraordinary disappearance of the Log books of officers in the ship.

It was according to naval rule that any so compiled should, at the expiration of the voyage, be deposited with the naval authorities. After a hundred years or so a number of *Endeavour* Logs were discovered behind some wainscotting at the Deptford Victualling Yard. They were safely conveyed to the good custody of the officers of the London Record Office, Chancery Lane. They could not have been seen by Dr. Hawkesworth any more than those of Cook himself.

The one by Lieutenant Hickes was kept from May 27, 1768, to March 14, 1771. Third Lieutenant Gore became Second Lieutenant March 26, 1770. Bootie's Log was from May 17, 1768, to September 3, 1770; Forward's, May 17, 1768, to September 26, 1770; Green, astronomer, September 24, 1763, to October 3, 1770; C. Clerke's, August 26, 1768, to October 3, 1770; Wilkinson's, June 22, 1768, to August 3, 1770; Pickersgill's, June 10, 1768, to September 29, 1770; Lieutenant Gore's from July 3, 1768, to December 7, 1769. An unsigned Log was from May 27, 1768, to September 28, 1770; a second from August 26, 1768, to July 15, 1769; a third, May 27, 1768, to September 28, 1770; and a fourth from May 27, 1768, to January 9, 1770.

George Nowell was Carpenter; Samuel Evans, Boatswain. The Quarter-master Thierman, and Widowson came from New York. James Magra, afterwards Matra, of New York, volunteered as seaman, but rose to be Midshipman, and the special friend, through many years, of Sir Joseph Banks, whose correspondence is in the Museum. Not one of the Deptford Logs knows *Botany Bay* or *New South Wales*.

How came these seamen's Logs hidden? Why was their testimony not to be forthcoming in the book? Had the discovery of the *Dauphin* Map, 1542, put *Stingray Bay* out of court, and induced the Editor, not Banks, nor Cook, to revive the ancient name of *Baie des Plantes*? Did Banks and Solander object to the removal of Cook's name, or were other and higher influences at work to conceal the Deptford Logs, so that all might hear only *Botany Bay* and *New South Wales*? But the Record Office has the Deptford hidden Logs, that came to tell another tale than that of the official publication.

BOTANY BAY.

LOG REFERENCES.

The Cook's *Museum Autograph Log*, 27,885, has this version of the visit to the Bay:—

"*Sunday, April 29, 1770.*—Gentle breezes and settled weather. At 3 p.m. anchored in 7 fathom water in a place which I call'd Sting-Ray Harbour, the South point bore S.E., and the North point East distant from the south shore 1 mile. We saw several of the natives on both sides of the Harbour as we came in, and a few hutts, women, and children on the north shore opposite to the place where we anchor'd, and where I soon after landed with a party of men, accompanied by Mr. Banks, Dr. Solander, and Tupia—as we approached the shore the natives all made off except two men, who at first seem'd resolved to oppose our landing. We endeavour'd to gain their consent to land by throwing them some nails, beeds, &c., ashore, but this had not the desired effect, for as we put into the shore one of them threw a large stone at us, and as soon as we landed they threw 2 darts at us, but the firing of two or three musquets loaded with small shott they took to the woods, and we saw them no more. We found here a few poor Hutts, made of the Bark of trees, in one of which were hid 4 or 5 Children, with whom we left some strings of Beeds, &c. After searching for fresh water without success except a little in a small hole—dug in the sand—we embarqued and went over to the north point of the Bay, where in coming in we saw several of the natives—but when we now landed we saw nobody, but we here found some fresh water, which came trinkling down and stood in Pools among the rocks, but as this was troublesome to get at I sent a party of men ashore in the morning abreast of the Ship to dig holes in the Sand, by which means we found fresh water, sufficient to water the Ship. After breakfast I sent some empty casks ashore to fill, and a party of men to cut Wood, and went myself in the Pinnace to sound and explore the Bay, in the doing of which I saw several of the natives, who all fled at my approach."

In reference to the name of Botany Bay, Cook's *Autograph Log*, numbered 27,885, Additional Manuscripts, British Museum, must have the first place. There we read:—

"Remarks on May the 6th, 1770." "Pleasent weather. People emp^d wooding," &c.

Afterwards came the Bay news, thus:—

"The Yawl return'd from fishing, having caught two Sting rays, whose weight was near 600 lbs. The great quantity of these sort of fish found in the place occasioned my giving it the name of *Sting-Ray Harbour*. Light airs and fair weather."

The *Endeavour* or Banks's Log, 8,959 of Museum, under date May 6, simply remarks: "Caught two Skeat whose weight was near 600 lbs."; but the ship left without naming the *Stingray* or Skeat Bay in this log.

The PALLISER Log, a direct present from Captain Cook to his old patron, Sir Hugh Palliser, and ever since preserved in the family, though not positively in Cook's handwriting, is signed by him, and must be ever considered of the highest authority. It knows nothing of *Botany Bay*.

Extracts from the Palliser Log.

Remarks, &c., in Stingray Harbour:—

"Gentle breezes and settled wea^r At 3 p.m. Anchor'd in 7 fa. water in a place which I called Sting-Ray Harbour, the S^o· point Bore S.E., and the N^o· p^t East Dist. from the S. Shore 1 Mile. We saw Severell of the Natives on both sides of the Harbour as we came in, and a few Hutts, women, and children, on the North Shore opposite the place were we anchor'd, and where I soon after Landed with a party of men, Accompanied by Mr. Banks, Dr. Sollander, and Tupia. As we approached the Shore the Natives all made off, except two men who at first seemed resolved to oppose our landing. We endeavour'd to gain there Consent to land by throwing them some Nails, Beeds &c. ashore, but this had not the desir'd effect but as we put in to the shore, one of them threw a Large stone at us and as soon as we landed they threw 2 darts at us but the Fireing of 2 or 3 musquets loaded with small shott they took to the woods and we saw them no more. We found here a few Old hutts made of the Bark of Trees in one of which were hid 4 or 5 children with whom we left some strings of beeds &c^a· After searching for fresh water, without Success Except a little in a small hole dug in the Sand we embarqued."

Remarks on Monday, 6 May, 1770:—

"The Yawl returnd from fishing having Caught 2 Stingrays the weight of which was near 600 lb. The great quantity of these sort of fish found here. Occasioned my giving it the Name of *Stingray Harbour*."

THE LIEUTENANT'S LOG AND STING REA BAY

The most reliable opinion as to matters connected with a voyage may be expected from the first mate or chief officer of a vessel. Lieutenant Zackary Hickes, whose log of the ship *Endeavour* was recovered a few years ago, gives his "Remarks on board his Majesty's Barque *Endeavour* New Holland, 1770." Therein we read for successive days:

> "Moor'd in Sting Rea Bay."

While there, on Sunday, April 29, he wrote:

> "Hoisted ye boats out, and ye Capn^n &c. attempting to land was opposed by a few of ye Natives who dispersed on being wounded with small shot. In y^e evening returned having found a watering place."

Zackary Hickes notes their leaving Sting Rea Bay, May 8th. Under latitude 34° 6" he writes:

> "Moored in *Sting Rea Bay* the mouth of the Bay from E. to N.E. ½ E. distant from the shore ¾ mile."

On May 17 his progress was "Sting ree bay 2° 00 E$^{t.}$" The Chief Officer knew nothing of Botany Bay.

RICH^D PICKERSGILL is the signature to what is called "A Logg of ye Proceedings, &c." He was master's mate for the ship. After stating on April 28:—

> "Moor'd in Sting ray Bay," it adds: "April 29. At 3 the Cap^n &c went ashore and were opposed on landing by 2 of the Nat^s whom they were obliged to sting with small shot which frighted them into ye woods."

On May 4 he notes "striking Stingerrays."

> "May 5, 1770—*Stingerray Bay* lies in Lat^d 34·06 S & Long^d W^t of Long^d on 20·43. It is form'd by two Low P^{ts} between which their is a passage of one mile with 12 f^{ms} water on the E^t side lies a Little Island and off ye S^o end of it is a Shore where the Sea some times Breaks after you are in the Bay spreads and tends to ye w^t ward for about 6 or 7 Miles and then ends in two large Lagoons off the S^o shores lies large flats with only 6 & 7 feet water upon them is a great Quantity of Stingerrays the Bay is very Shole but there is a Channel which lies open to ye entrance with 5 and 6 f^m water, but after you are two miles within it sholes to 3 the Bay is about 4 Miles Broad and has a regular tide. The Country is very rich and fertile and has a fine appear^{ce} we saw a large tree which grows allone and yealds a Gum like Dragons Blood this we found in great Quantitys sticking to ye Bark the Tree on which it grows is very large & spreads, but does not grow Stright nor tall besides we saw a wood which has a grain like oak and would be very du-

rable if used for Building the leaves are like a Pine leaf the Soil is a light sandy black earth mix'd but is very shallow upon digging we found vast Quantitys of Oyster Shells which seem'd to have been underground a great while We also found a Tree which bore a red berry about ye size of a Cherry, but they grew only in one Place — the inhabitants are so shy that we had no kind of Intercous with them they us'd to come down every evening arm'd with Lances and wooden Swords they appeard very thin and had their faces Daub'd over with some thing white one day as the Surgeon was walking in the woods which is all clear of under wood he had a Lance hove at him out of a tree but the man made of this was all we saw of them except when they were fishing off in their canoes which are very small & made of Bark they carry one man who paddles with two small pieces of wood they use them in striking fish on ye flats their Houses are several Pieces of Bark sett up against an other & open at each end and are the worst I ever saw the people have nothing to cover themselves but go quite naked men & women, and are the most wretched sett I ever beheld or heard of."

Green's Log is by the astronomer of the expedition. He heads his page "Coasting New Holland northward." Though he puts April 28 for 29, his Botany Bay visit is thus recorded: —

"Hoisted out the boats at 3 the Cap^{tn} &c. with Marines and boat's crew arm'd attempted landing but were opposed on the rocks of Sandy beach by 2 Indians with 4 prong'd wooden fish gigs tipt at the ends with 4 fish bones and fastened to ye wood with a gummy resinous substance; one of them under cover of a shield approach'd the boats and threw his Gig and in return was wounded with small shot. They now fled & with them a woman and 6 or 7 boys.

"On the beach they found 3 or 4 canoes made of the bark of a tree gather'd up at either end and stuck open with a few sticks for thwarts — the houses too (about 5) were no more than angular Kennels made by binding a piece of bark in the middle and resting either end on the ground encreasing the N^o of the pieces of bark according to ye length desired."

An *unnamed* log has the same account of the Bay.

The *Log* signed *Cha Clerke* is, like others of the early Cook age, wholly innocent of a reference to *Botany Bay*.

This is its treatment of April 29th: —

"Moored in *Sting Rea* bay. Little wind and fair. ½ past 1 came too with ye B.B. in 6½ fa sandy ground hoisted ye boats out. The Cap &c. attempting to Land was opposed by a few natives who dispersed on being wounded by small shot, in ye evening they returned having found a watering place."

On Saturday, May 5, we read: —

"Moored in Sting Rea Bay."

The WILKINSON's Log ranges from June 22, 1768, to August 3, 1770. Under April 29 we have this report: —

"Little wind and fair W ½ past 1 came too with the Bower in 6½ fm water, sandy ground. Hoisted out the Boats at 3 P.M. the Capt and Mr. Banks and Dr. Sollander went on Shore and was Opposed by the Natives at their landing on account the Captain was obledg to Sting one with Small Shot. After they all retired to the woods in the Evening the Cap[t] having found a watering place" &c.

On May 5 is recorded: —

"Moored in *Stingray Bay*, New Holland."

In "A Logg of the Proceedings of His Majesty's barque *Endeavour*," commencing May 27, 1768, to September 26, 1770, *Step[n] Forwood*, gunner, writes: —

"*Remarks on Sting Ray Bay New Holland.* Little wind and fair weather ½ past 1 came too with B[n] B[r] in 6½ fath[m] water Sandy ground. Hoisted out the Boats and the Cap[t] and Gentlemen went on Shore but were Opposed in landing by two Indians standing on the Shore with their Spears in their Hands Ready to heave at the Boat. Notwithstanding the Cap[t] tried all Means to Perswaid them to Lay their wapons down by Heaving them on shore Presents but all to no purpose. At last finding Nothing would do the Cap[t] fired a Load of small Shott at them which so frightend them that they Run into the woods After finding a watering Place the boats returned."

An unsigned Log of the *Endeavour* was kept from August 26, 1768, to September 28, 1770. Its account of the Bay entered April 29 was: —

"Little wind & fair wea[r] ½ past 1 came too with the B[t] Bower in 6½ fam Sandy Ground. Hoisting the Boats out at 3 the Captain and Mr. Banks & Dr. Sollander went on shore. They were opposed in attempting to land by some of the Natives whom they were obliged to sting with some shotts which frightened them in to the woods — in the Evening the Capt[n] Returnd having found a watering Place."

The Log in the possession of the Admiralty, differing only in the inferiority of writing from that called the *Queen's Log*, is similar to others and later so-called Cook's copies.

Neither of them cites the first named *Stingray* or *Sting Rea* Bay. But the Admiralty Log records two sorts of trees there, one hard, heavy and black like *Lignum Vitæ*, and the other "tall and straight something like Pines."

Then follows:

> "The great quantity of new plants &c. Mr. Banks & Dr. Solander collected in this place occasioned my giving it the name Botany Bay it is situated in the Lat^{de} 34°. 11 S. Long 208°."

The Admiralty Log notes what none of the old Cook's Logs knew.

> "Abreast of a Bay or Harbour wherein there appeared to be safe anchorage which I called Port Jackson it lies 3 Legs to the northw^d of Botany Bay."

Other Logs only notice it as an inlet, but add no name.

CORNER'S LOG.

Around this production the battle has raged awhile. As it was exposed for sale more than once, failing to attract attention, and had evidently been manipulated, suspicion was naturally excited, and one well known official expert assured me it was practically worthless. A bad impression was made by the assertion of Mr. Corner that the *Log* was in Cook's handwriting. As the Record Office, as well as the British Museum, could show a number of Cook's own letters, official and private, experts could not be deceived.

It may, nevertheless, have proceeded from the same source as some others of a later date, as that one in Royal Possession, and the one in the keeping of the Admiralty. In fact, the latter is very similar in its text to *Corner's* Log, always excepting the reference to *Botany Bay* instead of Cook's own appellation of *Stingray Harbour*, and the insertion of the name of *New South Wales*, or *New Wales*, instead of the total absence of those words in ALL the Logs of Cook and his officers.

It was evident to me, as to others, that several copies, more or less similar, had been sent to England after the last day's record in any *Log* upon leaving New Holland, the name of which is alone the heading of any page of a *Log*.

I have not seen the so-called *Queen's* Log, but any one who examined *Corner's* Log, as many did, would see that it came here originally with blank spaces for certain days, and others were vacant to receive the proper names of places, which had, it is to be presumed, to be added in this country!!

It is, however, not a little puzzling to find that Cook, who is *reported* to have sent these copies from Batavia, while staying there, should have allowed a copy for the Admiralty to go off with New South Wales as the name of the new territory, and send another (Corner's) bearing the denomination of New Wales. Still more extraordinary that Cook's own well ascertained *Logs*, two in the British Museum and one at Sunderland—the only ones extant—should have neither *New South Wales*, *New Wales*, nor *Botany Bay* mentioned.

The knowledge of such circumstances might well have caused experts to entertain doubts.

I had this hawked-about *Log* in my possession, and took tracings of portions, satisfying a well-known historian, and valued public officer at the Record Office, that the Log before us had been tampered with.

Although one of the empty spaces had, as in other cases, been filled up, in a handwriting different from that in the text, as *Port Jackson*, which never appears in the Logs of Cook and his officers, it was easy to suppose it referred to a Secretary to the Admiralty, Sir George Jackson, afterwards recognised as Sir George Duckett, the great friend to Bishop Stortford.

Erasures and re-writing are not confined to *Botany Bay. Rockingham Bay* has evidently had two earlier changes. Halifax Bay has similarly suffered. If adopted, as some fancy, as the Log used by Dr. Hawkesworth, considerable freedom was used.

The signatures to all Cook's genuine logs and copies is *Jam^s Cook*, with a grand flourish; but Corner's has *James Cook* only.

CORNER AND BOTANY BAY.

Corner's Log, having been re-written, corrected in spelling, &c., and afterwards printed and circulated as a veritable Cook's Log, what it had to say about *Botany Bay* may reasonably excite the deepest interest and attention.

In various Logs, elsewhere described, the Bay has been called *Sting Rea* or *Ray Harbour*, and the reason stated in Cook's own words, and those of his chief officer, was on account of the numbers of the fish *Stingray*, *Skeats*, or *Skate*.

Corner's, May 6th, says, on the contrary:

> "The great quantity of *plants* Mr. Banks and Dr. Solander found in this place occasioned my giving it the name of *Botany Bay*."

On May 30th we read of:

> "The same sort of Water Fowl as we saw in *Botany Bay*."

We cannot avoid expressing surprise at finding that the gentleman whose duty it was to fill up the vacant spaces, purposely left open for the insertion of names of places, was not always correct in orthography. He may have intended always to write *Botany*, but varied it in *Bottany, Bottony, Bottonest, Botony, Botanist*.

He is not sure even when describing "which I called *Port Jackson*" as he is led to write, "it lies 3 Leag^s to the Northw^d of *Botóny Bay*."

When, however, we come carefully to examine the full original paragraph about Botany Bay, we seem to understand the mode of action. The alteration was not made by the first copyist of the *Log*, nor by one particular person afterwards. There may have been some doubt even then about the settlement, or else why the erasure of one way of spelling, the substitution of another, and even traces of further erasure before final arrangement of name.

It was this that excited my suspicions. I was very candid in statement to some officials at the Admiralty of my honest belief that there had been some foul play in London. Later on, when I had again, with others, looked at the real journals in the

British Museum, regarded, and copied, the *Logs* found at the Deptford Victualling Yard, and especially had made personal inspection for three days at Sunderland of a Log given by Cook himself to his old Admiral, Sir Hugh Palliser, my doubts of this Log were confirmed.

Let us now refer to the original Corner's Log, transported by purchase from Mr. Corner, to New South Wales, where, if not further affected, it will be seen as I state.

If the reader mentally divide the Botany Bay story, under May 6, he will discover first the usual Log transcriber. In the space which he left, *by somebody's order*, he would perceive quite a different hand ("plants Mr. Banks and Dr. Solander"). Then returns the first hand, "found in this place occasioned my giving it the name of" — —. Another space is filled with a half erased second-hand "Botóny" followed by the word in original *"bay."*

In a tracing I took some years ago, under head of May 6, I read: "appeared to be safe anchorage which I called" (in original hand); but in the space adjoining, in the second hand I read: *"Port Jackson."* Then, as usual, the first resumed: "it lies 3 Leag^s to the Northw^d of." After a space, or, rather, within the space, is a bungling *"Bottony"* Bay.

Under May 13 we read: "we found (in the space) *Bottonist* Harbour." Eight lines lower, though in distinctly altered form, we read: "saw at *Botany* Harbour."

How different all this from the unaltered, unspaced account by the Captain's copy, given by himself to Sir Hugh Palliser, in which it only says: "The great Quantity of these sort of fish found here occasion'd my giving it the name of Stingray Harbour"!

So it is hardly correct to say, "It is, however, called *Botany Bay* from the first in the Journals," any more than "No autograph Journal is, so far as is known, in existence."

The fact of this "Corner's Log" becoming another ground for the publication of one, or many more, *"Cook's Endeavour,"* can arise only from the supposition of its likeness to the so-called *"Queen's Log"* and *"Admiralty Log."* But these, admitted to be copies, cannot compare with the one personally sent by Cook, with his signature, to Palliser, or that sent to the British Museum as Cook's by his companion on the voyage, Sir Joseph Banks; or, far more, that in Cook's *own hand* and *signature*, as seen in his own official letters.

Yet this Harbour was placed on a French map, dating from the reign of our Henry VIII, as *Baie des Herbages.*

Geographers have not been the most reticent upon the singularity and apparent after-thought of the name *Botany Bay*. It was hardly to be expected that Cook, though a skilled draftsman and interested in charts, would trouble himself about old *Mappemondes*, dealing with localities that were scarcely likely to come in his way, or, at any rate, until his appointment to observe the Transit of Venus in the Northern Pacific; yet he was not ignorant of what French navigators had done. In the British Museum one may see his translation of a French Voyage from Havre up the St. Lawrence. This copy is dated 1755. He may, therefore, be credited with the knowledge of French Mappemondes before the Fronde Civil Wars; in which charts, parts, at least, of Australia were delineated, and of dates anterior to Dutch movements.

The *Gazette Nationale* of February 11, 1807, discusses the question as to the possibility of Cook making acquaintance of a celebrated map in London, before the *Endeavour* sailed in August, 1768.

That wonderful and precious *Dauphin Mappemonde*, which I have seen at the Museum, dating from 1542, might not have been known to non-scientific Englishmen, but found a home at last in our Museum. Was Dr. Solander, Cook's botanical fellow-voyager, curator at the Museum when it arrived there? Were he or his friend Banks aware of its existence, or only learnt of it after their return? On that Map the *whole* eastern coast of New Holland, afterwards known as New South Wales, is laid down distinctly.

In that case, there was no marvel in Cook's striking from New Zealand, in a *direct* line to the southern extremity of that coast, at Cape Howe, and following the shore northward, instead of seeking a connection with the Dutch Nuyt's discovery to the south-west. He would be going over the old waters traversed by the ships from Spain and Portugal.

That gorgeous Dauphin map had its places marked in a sort of Frenchified Portuguese, as if a Dieppe cartographer had not got hold of the right words, or had, for a purpose, disguised them. Thereon, however, we read "coste dangerouse" about the spot where Cook was afterwards wrecked, as well as *Baie des Plantes* on the site of our *Botany Bay*.

The *Gazette Nationale* writer notes that the *Dauphin* map, marked with the Arms of France, was discovered, by chance, in the house of a private person, and asks if the news of it could have reached the Dutch, and so got known to a few English before its real presence in London about 1767, it not being there in 1766.

Referring to the Librarian, Solander, the French critic of 1807 adds: "That the denomination of *Baie des Plantes*, which he had read upon the Map confided to him, might be a fresh stimulus in the hope of botanizing on this unknown coast, since the memory of it no longer existed, and particularly in a place designated by a name so attractive to him."

It is curious that Cook gave Solander's name to the south point of the bay, "as if," says the French writer, "he were pleased to compliment his botanical friend, on perceiving at length this land, the object of his desires, where since it was already named the *Bay of Plants*, he must have hoped to reap an ample harvest."

Yet the secret, if so, was well kept till *after* the voyage of the *Endeavour*, since then *only* did the name of *Botany Bay* appear in Dr. Hawkesworth's work. In all Cook's old *Logs* we see merely *Stingray* or *Skeat Bay*, and similarly in *all* the Logs or journals of the chief officers and the petty officers.

Or, had Dr. Hawkesworth, Cook, Banks and Solander meanwhile made acquaintance with the appellation of *Baie des Plantes* and appropriated it for history? This theory would account for the various alterations of *Botany* on Corner's Log.

THE TAKING POSSESSION
OF THE TERRITORY.

The variations upon this subject are very remarkable.

Without noting what is contained in the so-called "Official History" of the "Voyage in the *Endeavour*," it must be allowed that *reported Logs* of Cook, now in the possession of the Sovereign and the Admiralty, give the general statement that Possession of the Territory was taken by Cook, after leaving the eastern side of New Holland, in the usual form, in the name of the King, as NEW SOUTH WALES. By that name Dr. Hawkesworth publicly acknowledges the country in his work; and by that name it has since been known. It is so seen in the Admiralty Log, though Corner calls it *New Wales*.

The official story of taking Possession, as given by Dr. Hawkesworth, is as follows:

> "As we were now about to quit the eastern coast of New Holland, which I had coasted from latitude 38° to this place, and which I am confident no European had ever seen before, I once more hoisted English colours, and although I had already taken possession of several particular parts, I now took possession of the whole eastern coast from latitude 38° to this place, lat. 10° 55" , in right of His Majesty King George the Third, by the name of NEW SOUTH WALES, with all the bays, harbours, rivers and Islands situated upon it; we then fired three vollies of small arms, which were answered by the same number from the ship. Having performed this ceremony upon the Island, which we called POSSESSION ISLAND, we re-embarked in our boat, but a rapid ebb tide setting NE made our return to the vessel very difficult and tedious."

The Admiralty Log contains, like some other later journals, this version:—

> "I now once more hoisted English Colours and in the name of His Maj^y King George the Third took Possession of the whole Eastern Coast from the above Lat$^{de.}$ down to this place by the name of NEW SOUTH WALES together with all the Bays Harbours Rivers and Islands situate upon the said Coast upon which we fir'd 3 Volleys of Small arms which were answer'd by the like number from the ship."

Although Corner's Log resembles the Admiralty one so nearly, being one among several copies made while Cook was staying to refresh in Java, yet it, curiously enough, calls the land New Wales, which according to me would give the copy some priority to other copies thence.

Corner's Log has this story of the Possession:

> "The Eastern Coast from the sea of 38°.1" down to this place, I am confident was never seen or visited by any European power before us and notwithstanding I had in the name of his Maj[y] taken possession of several places on this coast, I now once more hoisting colours in the name of His Maj. King George the Third took Possession of the whole Eastern Coast from the above lat[de.] down to this place by the Name of New Wales, together with all the Bays."

This log, therefore, commits Cook to the distinct affirmation that he was the first European who had either seen or visited any part of that eastern coast. He effectually disposes of the claims of Dutch, Spanish and Portuguese navigators.

Before dismissing this log, I would call attention to a notable observation on the margin of one page, which I recognised to be in Cook's own handwriting, and which, though no evidence of the log itself having been composed by the Captain, must be reported as once having been in his hand, at some time or other. Here are the words:

> "This day I restore Mr. Magra to his duty as I did not find him guilty of the crimes laid to his charge."

The *crimes* consisted in some ridicule of Orton, the Captain's clerk, when exhibiting himself in a state of intoxication. Magra, or rather Matra, a gentleman volunteering for the voyage as a seaman, had, upon the discovery of his ability, enforced by the active recommendation of Mr. Banks, been made a midshipman, from which position he had been degraded for a few days on account of the part he was known to have taken in this frolic.

It is interesting and important here to note that this very James Matra, travelling companion with Mr. (afterwards Sir Joseph) Banks, was the *direct instrument* of the establishment of the English Colony of New South Wales. He, encouraged by Banks, petitioned the Ministry that the land, even then recognized as New South Wales, should be appropriated as a colony for English settlers in America, who had lost their all in supporting the English Government against the American rebels. Mr. Pitt, however, preferred a settlement of persons taken from overcrowded English gaols.

This log incorrectly signs the Captain's name as *James* Cook, not *Jam[s]*, the correct way, so continuously used by himself.

An unnamed Deptford Log has this reference to the taking possession on Wednesday, August 22, 1770:—

> "At 6 Possession was taken of this country in his Maj[s.] Name &c. by hoisting a Jack on shore, this was announced from the Ship with colours flying; the whole concluded with 3 cheers."

The astronomer, Mr. Green, is satisfied to copy Pickersgill, saying:—

> "At 6 Possession was taken of this country in his Majesty's Name &c.; this was announced from the shore by Vollies and answered from on b[d.] Colours flying and concluding with 3 cheers."

One Log, unsigned by the writer, has a description of taking possession in similar terms to those evidently prepared on the voyage, saying:—

> "Aug. 22. The pinnace and yawl with the capt[n.] and gentlemen went on shore to examine the contry and view the Coast. from one of the Hills some time after saw some Turtle. At 6 Possession was taken of this contry in his Majesty's Name and under his Colours, fired severell volleyes of small arms on y[e] Occasion and cheard 3 Times which was answ[d.] from y[e] ship".

Gunner Forwood has a short story on Possession:—

> "The Capt[n.] took Possession of the country in his Majesty's Name &c. This was announced from the shore Vollies Fired and Colours flying from on board with D[o.] concluding with 3 cheers."

John Bootie's Log treats the Possession narrative in the exact terms of another, saying:—

> "August 22. At 6 possession was taken of this locality in his Majesty's Name &c. This was announced from the shore by Vollies and answered from on b[d.] with Colours flying and concluding with 3 Cheers."

Here, again, as in the other cases, the words "New South Wales" do not occur.

The *Palliser* or *Sunderland* Log of Mr. Hudson's may be quoted:—

> "Betwixt these two points we could see no land, so that we were in great hopes we had found a passage into the India Sea, but in order to be a little inform'd I landed with a party of men on the Island which lays on the right side of the Passage where from a hill I could see no lands in the above direction Before and after we anchor'd we saw many of the Natives upon this Island, but they all fled upon my landing—a little before Sun sett I took Possession of the country in His Majesty's Name, and fired a volley of small arms on the occasion, which was answered from the ship."

On this *Possession* subject we have the weightiest authority, Cook's *autograph Log, Museum Catalogue*, 27,885 for August 22, when leaving the Australian coast:—

> "We were in great hopes that we had found a passage into the India Sea but in order to be better inform'd I landed with a Party of men on the Island which lays to the S.E. side of the Passage where from a hill saw no land in the above direction. Before and after we anchor'd we saw a good many of the Natives upon this Island but they all fled upon my landing. A little before sunsett I took possession of the Country in His Majesty's name and fired

3 Volleys of small arms on the occasion which was answerd from the ship. High water at 4 o'clock," &c.

Banks's Log (of Cook), 8959 of Museum Catalogue, remarked:—

"The Pinnace and Yawl with the Capt[n.] and gentlemen went on shore to Examine the Country and view the Coast from one of the Hills soon after saw some Turtle. It was high water. When we came too the Tide of Ebb set from the S.W. 5k. 2m. per hour. At 6 possession was taken of this Country in his Majesty's name and under his Colours fired several volleys of small arms on the occasion and cheer'd 3 times which was answer'd from the ship."

In each case of Cook's real *Logs* no name of any kind would appear to have been selected for the country, else, in all probability, it would have been stated in one or in both Logs.

The Chief Officer, Lieut. Hickes, knew nothing of taking possession of the land in the King's name as *New South Wales*.

His Log for August 21 refers to Chacho Harbour:

"Wednesday 22. Latt. 10° 45" Long, made W. from y[e] Straits 00° 13. These Straits are in Longitude 142° 25 E[t.] The Capt[n.] went on shore, hoisted y[e] Colours and took possession of y[e] Country for y[e] King, fired several volleys and cheered 3 times which was answered from y[e] Ship, at 10 a.m. slack water weighed and made sail."

The Log of *Richard Pickersgill* gives this short version, imitating or being imitated:—

"At 6 *Possession* was taken of this country in his Majesty's Name and this was announced from the shore by Vollies and answer'd from on b[d.] Colours flying and concluding with 3 cheers."

The *Cook's Log* presented by Sir Joseph Banks to the British Museum, and catalogued therein as 8959, is the most important of what Logs I, as an archivist, would regard the genuine Cook's, as it was sanctioned by the authority of a fellow voyager.

The quotation from this Log, on the taking possession of the territory, runs thus:—

"Mod. and clear wea[r.] saw a number of smoaks along shore at 1 Lay too for the yawl, Pinnace and Longboat, Sounding ½ p[t.] 2 made sail and steer'd for a passage, Between some Islands and the Main at 3 fired a gun and made the Signell for the Boats to sound the next Passage, to the N.ward of the above Mention'd ¾ p[t.] 3 was in the Passage Dist[ce.] from Each shore ¾ of a mile—saw several Indians who follow'd us shouting. At 4 fir'd a gun and made the Signell for the Boats. Came too with the B[t.] Bower in 6¾ fa[m.] good ground Veer'd to ½ a Cable. Ext^{e} of the Land on the East side No. 56 E^{t} an Island to S.W. the Main on the W^{t} side from N.S.E. to S. 73 W^{t} 8 miles Dist^{ce} from the Eastern shore One mile. The Pinnace and yawl with the Captn and Gentlemen went on shore to Examin the Country and view the Coast from one of the Hills. Soon after saw some Turtle it was high water. When we came too, the Tide of Ebb set from the S.W. 3k. 2m. p^{r} Hour, at 6 possession was taken of this Country in his majesty's name and under his Coulours Fired several volleys of small arms on the occasion and Cheer'd 3 times, which was answer'd from the ship."

There is, therefore, in the most orthodox Logs of H.M.S. *Endeavour*, not any authority for the names of *Botany Bay* and *New South Wales*.

END.

In a capital sketch of Captain Cook, appearing in the Sydney *Town and Country Journal* on February 22, 1879, when the noble New South Wales statue to Captain Cook was unveiled, the writer observed, "what the legendary Æneas was to Rome, Captain James Cook is to Eastern Australia."

Though the remark only referred to the remarkable wanderings by both men over various seas, the word *legendary* may, in a way, be applied to the two. The voyage of the *Trojan* has been regarded by the learned men of Europe as mythical, or, at least, explanatory of shifting reckonings of time, or to such groupings of constellations as should elucidate human fancies, and the inventions of quasi-historians.

Æneas was but a poetical creation, and Cook was a living hero of the ocean. Yet, around the narratives of Cook's first southern voyage, when he was said to have discovered Eastern Australia, have gathered so many mysteries, as almost to give them the colour of myths.

Suspicions regarding the official account of the voyage arose at an early date. It leaked out, from those who had accompanied Cook, that the recorded official Admiralty narrative did not agree with their recollection of the several facts. The death of the author soon after the issue of his work increased the embarrassment as to the source of the materials from which he made his compilation. The second of Cook's voyages, so ably described by the Dean of Windsor, had the advantage of genuine logs, together with the presence and active assistance of the navigator himself. It unfortunately happened that most of the actors in the first or New Holland voyage were out of reach for questions whilst the story was being written.

Dr. Hawkesworth meant to prepare as interesting a narrative as he could, and tried to please home parties as flatteringly as circumstances permitted. Thus, men of science would be gratified by the selection of the place as *Botany Bay*, an Admiralty officer would be glad of the adoption of his name in *Port Jackson*, while the Dutch appellation of *New Holland* gave place to the more British one of *New South Wales*. Even *Torres Strait*, that honoured the navigators of Spain and Portugal, surrendered to the English name of *Endeavour Strait*.

The value of Cook's second voyage in the *Resolution*, which was brought out by the Dean of Windsor, had the advantage of good logs, with the presence of Captain Cook at its revision, and was, consequently, never questioned as that of the *Endeavour* had been under the editorship of Dr. Hawkesworth, which had a far more novel and romantic story to tell.

In a remarkable letter to Sir Joseph Banks by John Frederick Schiller, German translator of Hawkesworth's voyage, and dated November 14, 1773, the writer expresses the deep concern of a German bookseller at the wrong done to the sale of this translation by some published remarks in England, impugning the correctness of the official Admiralty narrative. He therefore seeks "some lines" from Sir Joseph, as Cook's fellow voyager, in refutation of those injurious assertions. The German scholar adds: "Mr. Ferber, an eminent mineralogist, says he has of late made a literary tour through Europe, and after his return from England asserted at Berlin that

> "Not only the respective Commanders, Messrs. Biron, Wallis, Carteret, &c., had publicly protested against Dr. Hawkesworth's account of their voyages, as containing misrepresented facts, but also that especially Messrs. Banks and Solander had publicly declared that they had never delivered any Papers of theirs into that Editor's hands, and that the Public was to wait for their own narrative, which was to be published within 3 or 4 years."

Mr. Schiller goes on to say: "In order to support these assertions, Mr. Ferber is said to have produced a letter which he affirmed to have received from Mr. Banks, and in which all these assertions are plainly expressed and corroborated."

If, then, suspicions were excited immediately after the publication of our authorised and popular version of Cook's voyage, it is not surprising that further investigation, as now made, should develop renewed scepticism. The recent record of the London Press that the Corner's Log had been pronounced by the Admiralty experts to be genuine, and in Cook's own handwriting, might well puzzle outsiders.

Had Sir Joseph Banks publicly answered the appeal of Mr. Schiller in 1773, and satisfied the world as to the authenticity of Dr. Hawkesworth's story, the necessity of any subsequent controversy might have been avoided. In that appeal to Banks and Solander "in the cause of Truth, of Justice, of Honour and Humanity," we read that the two naturalists "intend to publish in five or six years hence, in sixteen or eighteen folios and two thousand copper plates, and totally unconnected with Dr. Hawkesworth's narrative." Such a great work did not appear. Why not? History does not tell.

There has been sufficient reason for the present writer's long silence upon this inquiry, and particularly since he had reported on Cook's logs some six years ago.

Now, however, as the acting archivist is just entering his eighty-fifth year, Colonial friends here deemed it a proper time for the printing of this pamphlet in the cause of Truth, Justice, and Honour, it being his last contribution to Colonial history, the series of which began in 1845 by the publication of his *Geography for Australian Youth*, which was the first production, by the Australian Press, of any *Geography of Australia*.

JAMES BONWICK.

Norwood, *July 8, 1901.*

Lector House believes that a society develops through a two-fold approach of continuous learning and adaptation, which is derived from the study of classic literary works spread across the historic timeline of literature records. Therefore, we aim at reviving, repairing and redeveloping all those inaccessible or damaged but historically as well as culturally important literature across subjects so that the future generations may have an opportunity to study and learn from past works to embark upon a journey of creating a better future.

This book is a result of an effort made by Lector House towards making a contribution to the preservation and repair of original ancient works which might hold historical significance to the approach of continuous learning across subjects.

HAPPY READING & LEARNING!

LECTOR HOUSE LLP
E-MAIL: info@lectorhouse.com

9 789356 146297